CAREGIVERS

Reflections on Coping with Caregiving

Marlene Halpin

Islewest
PUBLISHING

Photography and Text
by Marlene Halpin, O.P., Ph.D.

Book Team
Publisher: Sandra J. Hirstein
Managing Editor: Mary Jo Graham
Assistant Editor: Sharon Cruse
Designer: Veronica Burnett

Copyright (c) 1998 by Islewest Publishing,
A division of Carlisle Communications, Inc.
4242 Chavenelle Road
Dubuque, IA 52002

Manufactured in the United States of America
All rights reserved.
ISBN 1-888461-05-5

Dedication

To my four o'clock friend . . .
To Joyce Underkofler
Who lives with exceptional graciousness
The meaning of caregiving

Contents

Foreword

What, ME a JUGGLER?
"You'd better believe it!
What's more, what I'm juggling are *bowling balls!*
There's not a light weight among them!"
She is dead serious, this wife, mother of three, career woman, who is now responsible for a parent no longer able to function independently.

"How many balls can you be expected to keep in the air at once," she demands, "and have some sort of balance in your own life?" Smart lady. *Balance* is what all of us need if we are to be much good to ourselves and others.

Easier said than done.

"There are *my* body's health needs; *my* emotional fulfillment; *my* soul's yearnings. The same is true of my husband and my children. Their concerns and their experiences need to be shared. It takes time and energy-and I love giving it to them. (Most times.)

"What about my home? Cleaning, food shopping, doing laundry. Making order out of chaos. The garden. Ordinary maintenance and repairs. Taking care of finances. The children's wants and needs. School. Sports. In addition, there are the people at work, and now there are my parents who really are in need. It's not only that they are in need, they hate being in need. The way they behave about being needy takes *more time* and energy to make a decent response.

"Balance! *How* does one achieve it? *Can* it be done at a time like this?"

These questions hang heavy on caregivers' hearts. No matter if the one needing care is a parent, spouse, lover, child or a special friend-the demands are new and must be fitted into an already full life.

When faced with something unpleasant, a little four-year-old boy said, *"I'd like to fast-forward this part."* Wouldn't we all! Yet that probably would be a mistake because the demands have so much to teach us.

The reflections in this book are offered in hope that you may learn how to find an acceptable balance deep within you.

Introduction

It's No Secret

Caregiving is no secret. For most of us it was a "taken for granted" sort of thing. Normally, children are taken care of, and so are those who get sick. It is all part of day-by-day living. So is the care given family members who have some disability. Those families have learned-and maybe taught-a great deal about caregiving and respect.

Today the word caregiving has an additional significance. Life expectancy keeps rising. Aging lasts longer. More older people need more care.

The time demanded from caregivers in the home varies from maybe an hour a day to being on call around the clock. Sometimes it simply involves checking that the person is all right; perhaps doing shopping or laundry. Sometimes more is involved: Taking care of bills. Scheduling appointments (and providing transportation). Monitoring medications. Sometimes more personal care is needed: help in dressing, shaving, and bathing. Hard decisions must be made-not always with everyone in agreement.

Such times often change the caregiver's life radically. They are times, often unexpected times, that force caregivers to take hard looks at themselves and their own values. Caregivers can turn into complainers, whiners, tight-lipped "do what is right-ers", victims insatiable for sympathy: any one of which is perfectly understandable. But these negative responses don't make for a good life.

Alternatively, caregivers can take these unexpected, unasked for situations as points of growth: of love, of greater maturity (even if in their 50's or 60's). Another level of love and intimacy can always happen. Another level of deep humanity can always be achieved.

There are so very many variables-whether in the illness or incapacity or in the attitudes of all involved-that caregiving is best viewed as a journey, perhaps an adventure, of the most personal sort.

May it be, in the long run, a deeply satisfying journey for the caregiver-and for everyone else involved.

Abandoned

Often I have read how
Chronically ill people feel *abandoned.*
It's so.

It's so, too,
That that's how I, a caregiver, feel!

I'm not free to go out.
>   *My friends give up asking me.*

I want to go, and I say yes, I shall.
Then I cancel.
>   *My friends don't "bother" me any more.*

I don't know any of the latest news about anyone.
>   *My friends don't call to exchange stories.*

I feel alone and isolated.
>   *My friends want more cheerful company.*

>   I think it's about time I had a talk with me.
>   I'm not stupid!
>   And–I AM alive!

What kind of deal
can I make with my friends
so that
we ALL are more gladsome?

Aggravation

Hospital? They won't keep her.
Nursing home? No!
Hospice? Not yet.

I could not manager her care and my job
without the agency. But-

> I come home and find *this* isn't done,
> *that* was said;
> things are put away in the wrong places.

> Aggravation!
> That's what I come home to.
> Aggravation!

Then (sometimes) I wonder:
> Why am I so upset every day?
> Why do none of the aids satisfy me?
> What makes me so fussy?

The (occasionally) I wonder:
> Might it be-
> *I'd rather be caring for her myself and I can't?*
> *I'm jealous of the one who gets to spend time with her?*
> *I'm vexed by the intrusion into my privacy?*
> *Or-what?*

> > *Does this have to be the way*
> > *I keep learning about myself?*

> > On second thought,
> > What is it they say about rose gardens?

Alone

Some people come.
They make appropriate
sounds and faces.

Others have stopped coming.
The ones with whom I would
bowl, or go to a show, or have coffee.
I can't leave him long enough to do these things.

I am left alone.

Alone

watching his living the very end of his life;
seeing the look in his eyes.

Alone

adjusting to all that is required of me,
including seeing the look in his eyes.

Alone

with my exhaustion, pity, grief, love;
my resentment, fear, anger,
my *not wanting* to see the look in his eyes.

Alone

with feeling guilty.

Alone.

Must I be so alone?

I think not!
(at least, on a good day,
I think not!)

Angry!

I get so angry!

I get so angry
    at the way they
    talk to me!

"Gee, Sis, you're swell!
You're *good* at taking care of Dad."

"It's good you have the time ...
Not me ... I'm so busy!"

"Thank God you live near Dad!
I sure don't."

"You're a natural
the way you care for him."

    I just want to YELL at them:
        "What do you think I am?
        Chopped liver?"

    How they trivialize
        who I am
        how I am
        what it means to me
            (and mine)
        how it is for me ...
        and
        how very convenient for them.

        With it all,
        when I think about it,

        I do rather like
        who I am.

Bowling Balls

My job.
My job is demanding.
So are some of the people there,
to say nothing about down-sizing, layoffs, and
other "situations."

My family.
When I come home from work
everyone wants a piece of me.
I want them to, for I love them.

My friends.
They want time to do things together, too.
They have things to talk over, too.

Now ... *this.*
On top of taking care of the house, my family, and friends: *this.*
This alone could be a full time job.

I was juggling.
Now I'm juggling bowling balls.

> (Once I get my breath
> perhaps I can also learn
> to clown a bit!)

Buttons

Button, button,
      Who has the button?

Ma has.

Ma plays with her buttons
      by the hour.

      She unbuttons her blouse.
      She buttons her blouse.
           Over and over and over
           with a child-like intensity
           and pride in her success.

Ma.

      She's gone.
      She's here.

           No matter.
           I love her.

           And I try,
           I try very hard,
           to keep her dressed.

Childish

He gets so childish!
At his age—he gets so childish!

Attention-getting:
      noise-making
      bed soiling
      forgetting, muttering, face-making, spilling,
      annoying.
So—childish!

And I—
      Do I treat him as a naughty child?
      In my tiredness, am I being childish at *my* age?

How do I see through his childishness
      to what he (as does a child) needs
      but which he (unlike a child) has had,
            is accustomed to, and misses?

      How do I let him know that I know his need?
      (If, indeed, I do!)

Computers

"It's in the computer."
Is there no recourse from:
"It's in the computer"?

His surgeon canceled the operation.
The bill came.
I called and was told:
    "It's in the computer."

He was in the hospital. True.
He did not have a hysterectomy.
I called and was told:
    "It's in the computer."

She never was a patient in that facility.
The bill came.
I called and was told:
    "It's in the computer."

                Is there no recourse from:
                "It's in the computer"?

                    I handle it. Sort of.
                    How does it handle me?

Dare I?

Dare I think it?
  (Well, in unguarded moments I do.)

Dare I dwell on it?
  (I think it's better not to.)

Dare I admit it?
  (To whom?)

          Who would understand
                  that I love him, and
                  I am willing to take care of him, and
                  oh, so truly!-
                  I *hate* him!

I astound myself
at the bouquet in my heart-
          if one can call
          hatred, anger, resentment,
          and sheer frustrated exhaustion
a "bouquet."

          But those are the things
          which grow there these days. These nights.
          These endless days and nights.

To whom can I say it?
          (safely?)
Who might hear my hate with heart
          —for me
          —for him, too?

                  Hear it, and
                  maybe
                  help me into
                  healing growth?

"Dear"

"Take care of yourself, dear."
"Be sure you get enough sleep, dear."
"Are you eating well enough, dear?"

"I'm glad you've got a good-paying job, dear.
... You get to do all those interesting things, while
 I'm just here" (sigh).

Then it starts:

      the pains
      the annoyances
      the inabilities
      the fears
      the boredom
      the "used to be's"

And I,

Am I to comfort, console,
      make everything come out all right?

If I take his
      litany of "dears" seriously,
How can I also
      console him in
      his litany of sorrows?

Now that I think about it,
How might I console him?

(If I succeed, even a bit,
maybe we can laugh a little, too.)

Different

It's different
seeing her
so sick, listless,
helpless.

It's different
my taking
care of *her.*

It's different
my doing
her jobs
(as well as my own).

The most different of all, I think,
Is that she can do nothing for me.

She can't ...
can she?

Or might it be possible
she
is bringing forth from
me
qualities I didn't know I had?

Thank you!

Distancing

I see myself doing it.

Without thinking about it
        (at least not consciously),
I see me
        DISTANCING
myself from her.

Watching her dying
        tears me apart.
I'm distancing myself.

Missing her, already
        grieving her death,
I'm distancing myself.

Knowing she
        can no longer "be there"
        for me,
I'm distancing myself.

                I see myself doing it.
                So does she.

                Does it leave me content?

Do I?

Do I
put him into a nursing home?

He fears it so much.
      What will it do to him?

He has a collection of nursing home stories.
      He scares himself and makes himself miserable.

He keeps reminding me
      of all he sacrificed for me.
      (It's true. He did.)

Relatives, cronies, neighbors, doctors,
      all hear about me, and how
      he will "die there."

OH!

There is his increasing disorientation.
There is his painfully increasing physical disability.
There is genuine danger for him, here, now.
There is my limited time, energy, skill.

With whom
lovingly, intelligently, realistically,
can I sort out
my fears, guilt, embarrassment, sorrow?

Who will help me understand the melange of
manipulation, rationalization, terror?

How can I look at all the possibilities
and come to something which
will honor us both?

Will I find a
"with whom"?

Soon?

Do I Really Love Him?

How many times
    have I wondered:
Do I really love him?

When we squabbled about money,
When we disagreed about the children,
When he didn't understand,
When he ... did what he did,
I wondered:
        Is it worth it?
        Do I really love him?

No longer do I wonder.

I *know* I do.
I *know* my faithfulness, my loyalty,
        my love.

So does he,
and so do others.

It is a
        very good knowing.

(I don't think I ever quite liked myself so much before!)

Empty Nest

I love my children.
I love my home.
I love having an empty nest
      as they fly away
      to start on their own.

Now

No longer do I have
an empty next.

      The chicks I hatched
      are busy hatching their own.

      The ones
      who hatched me
      are back.

My full nest
      is busy in different ways-
      not helping to grow up
      but certainly helping to grow.

      Leaving the nest this time
      will be much more sacred.

Faith

Ever since I can remember
FAITH has been part of my life.

As a child,
        I went with my family to church.

As a parent,
        I brought my children to church..

For holy days and celebrations:
        Christmas, Easter,
        Baptisms, weddings, funerals,
        I went to church.

I went to church–
        and listened
        and prayed.

Now?
Now, in a brand new way,
I have to ask:

        Do I *mean* what I've been saying?
        Do I *believe* what I've been saying I believe?
        Do I *trust* what I've been trying to live?
        Do I?

Maybe
I'll have to dig down,
down deeper inside,
past even the emptiness
to
        where my faith really is,
        to know again what (and who)
        I believe in, hope in,
        and most of all, love.

For Sure

I used to know things **for sure.**
I used to know *who* I could count on.
I used to know *what* I could count on.
—at least I thought I did.
Now
How do I find two doctors who will agree?
Who will put an end to these endless tests?
these painful, expensive, experimental tests?
Is this treatment worth it? Is refusing this treatment worth it?
Should we pull the plug?
I don't know.

Uncertainty has come into my life.
A permanent guest, it seems-
an unexpected, uncomfortable, and unwelcome guest.

But maybe, just maybe
Uncertainly is an angel of God

Is there an Angel of Uncertainty being sent to us?

Freedom

Freedom,
> like fun,
> used to be part of my life.

Now
> I'm stuck
> with little-or no-
> time to spend.

Someone reminded my
> of concentration camp survivors.

> Did they take it
> "a day at a time?"

> No!
> (It's too much for me, too.)

> How did they survive?
> "For a few seconds",
> is what they said.

>> "For a few seconds"
>> their good memories came back

>> "For a few seconds"
>> they got hold of their attitude.

Taking it
"a day at a time"
is too much.

> "For a few seconds?"
> Probably I can manage that!

Getting Even

I never guessed
> what a multitude of vengeances
> dwell in his heart. And in mine.

I never realized
> how important "getting even" still is.
> At his age! And ... at mine!

> I forgot to bring something.
> He forgot to take the medicine.
> I cleaned up the mess.

> I went out to dinner last night.
> He wouldn't talk to me today.

> I didn't answer his mumbling soon enough.
> He soiled the bed again.

> The children had a party without him.
> He threw everything within his reach at the door.

> *How often does*
> *"getting even"*
> *make it even?*

Gloating

She *gloats.*
As frail as she is,
As worn out as she is,
As much care as we need give her,
She *gloats.*

When we her (adult) children gather,
She looks at us and
She *gloats.*

When the grandchildren gather,
She looks at them and
She *gloats.*

I never thought
a GLOATER
would warm my heart.

This one does!
Every time!

May I be so blessed
with my children
and with their children
that when I see them
(no matter what condition I'll be in)
I shall be so lovingly proud, that
I, too, shall *gloat!*

God Knows

God knows
>I do what I can.

Sometimes
>(most of the time)
>I surprise myself
>at how much I get done!

Sometimes
>I'm so out of sorts,
>it's less. Much less.

God knows.

>If God is God,
>I think,

>If God wants *me*
>>to do more,
>God should give me
>>"more"
>>to do it with.

>If God's content
>>with how much I get done,
>Well,
>why shouldn't I be?

>>As for what's not done,
>>*the hell with it!*

Helpless

It isn't easy to watch–
to watch someone you love
dying, it seems, endlessly.

Some days I think:
        "It can't get worse!"
        It can.
        It does.
        Still there is life.

All through it
        I stand by,
        helpless.

                Helpless
                to cure, to restore health,
                to make it like it was.

Helpless
        to love
        and let my love be felt?

Hardly!

How Do I Love You?

How do I love you?
> Let me count the ways ... .

When we were young
> the ways were
> tender, fresh,
> perhaps lovingly foolish,
> and we laughed together.

Now that we are old,
> I still ask:
> How do I love you?
> Let me count the ways ... .

> No less tender, fresh,
> perhaps lovingly foolish
> and our laughter has gentled into loving smiles.

>> How do I love you?
>> Let me count the ways!

WARNING
AN AERATION SYSTEM
CREATING OPEN WATER
AND THIN ICE IS IN USE
ON THIS LAKE   STAY
CLEAR OF MARKED AREA

-STATE LAW-
TAKE TRASH
WITH YOU

Hygiene

Oh, how careful we are
    of hygiene!
        —washing hands
        —brushing teeth
        —keeping the germs at bay

Oh, how careful we are
    of courtesy!
        Teaching our children to say:
        "Excuse me."
        "Please" and "Thank You."
        "I'm sorry" (even if they're not).

Oh, how careful we need be
    to give and to receive
    daily rations of:

"I'm sorry."
"Please forgive me."

    Hygiene of soul
    is as daily as
    hygiene of body
    and as inevitably needed.

        "I'm sorry."

        "Me, too."

I Don't Want To

I have a list of
"I don't want to's"

Today it is headed by:
I don't want to talk about it.

I *really* don't want to talk about it.

When I talk about it

It makes it more real.
It hurts more.
It makes me feel the hurt more.
It complicates the hurt-
the look in their eyes,
the comments they make,
the advice they give-
probably well meant-
but it complicates things.

It's bad enough as it is.
I need to protect myself.
I have the right to that, don't I?

Yet,
that bundle
of heavy things
lies heavy on my spirit.

May God see my heart.
May God see all the
"I don't want to talk about it's"

and

May God
heal my hurting heart.

I Have A Life

Well, I used to.

Now ...
Now no matter how I try,
there's not enough time to do everything.

It's all sheer drudgery,
and with it,
failure to satisfy anyone.
I'm bone weary in spirit and body.

Fun?
It's in the dictionary, I suppose.

Rest?
That's like time: there's never enough.

A Life?
Forget it!

*If I were really
my own best friend,
what might I whisper to me?
... and then?*

I Never Knew

I never knew
my mother
was like *that!*

I suppose
I got married myself
rather young.
And tended to forget.

Then we were so busy
      finishing school
      starting a family
      succeeding at work
that I never noticed.

When we (or she) visited,
my children said what they did.
I thought ...
        that's just the children speaking.
And told them to behave themselves.

Now we have to take care of her.
She lives among us.
        I never knew she was like *that!*

                I look at the
                "I told you so", and the
                "See what I mean?"
                faces of my family.

                        They tell me
                        what gruesome things
                        they will do to me
                        if I act this way
                        when I get old
                        or sick, and they must care for me.

                        They outdo each other
                        in the gruesome area.

It makes us laugh.
(It keeps mother guessing!)

I Never Used To

I could write a long list of
"I Never Used To's ..."

For instance:

- I never used to break appointments.
- I never used to be at home every night of the week.
- I never used to let my hair and nails go.
- I never missed a game.
- I never used to feel guilty all of the time.

I don't like it.

I happens to me.
(I let it happen?)

Why?

At first everything was new.
The changes, the accommodations,
        took me by surprise.
Some of it was a shock.
I resented some of it.
I am sorry about most of it.

It is the way it is.

Now, that the surprise part is over
Might I change some of it?
Might I handle it better?

*(Perhaps I could look at myself
in a mirror, grin at me,
and ask:
"Well?")*

It's Not Enough

It's not enough.

No matter I visit-every day.
No matter I take (or bring back) laundry-every day.
No matter I sit and listen-every day.

It's not enough.

I have my family.
I have my household.
I have my job.
I (used to) have a social life.
I **do** go and visit, **every** day.

It's not enough.

I can't help it if
it's not enough for her.

Honestly,
it is enough for me!

Isn't It A Shame!

"Isn't it a shame?"
        visitors exclaim,
"when you think of how she used to be!"

People nod in sad agreement.

                I want to shout at them:
                "No! It is not!"

Just as it is NOT a shame that
        —an infant no longer needs be carried,
        —a child no longer has to be buttoned and zipped,
        —an adolescent no longer has to be driven
        —an adult no longer has to receive an allowance

So it is NOT a shame
        that one grows old, or ill, or both.

                If one lives long enough
                that is normal.

                Not only is it not shameful,
                but it gives us the chance,
                in our caring, to say
                in unmistakable terms:

                        You are a worthy human being.
                                -not for what you might grow up to be
                                -not for what you can do

                        but

                        BECAUSE YOU ARE!

You, me, all of us CAN
learn a better meaning of
human dignity.

Journey

It used to be easy,
      exciting, even,
to hear:
    Life is a journey,
    not a destination.

My journey was well
    and happily planned.
It didn't all happen,
    but much of it did.
I've had a good life.

    Then someone threw the switch.
    My train was put on another track.

    Here I am.

    A caregiver.

Me! A caregiver!

> My time is not my own.
> My plans are not my own.
>
> My skills are growing-
> > in ways not of my preference.
> My priorities are changing.
> My habits are modified.
> My interests are ... in the background.

Why?

Why does it have to be this way?

Why does my journey take me into *these* valleys?
> (They were not mentioned in my itinerary.)

> > Do I believe there is a reason?
> > *If so, do I have to know it?*

Just Suppose

Just suppose
        he does what he threatens to do?

Just suppose he
        never makes another appointment
        or sees another waiting room
        or never, ever, goes back inside?

Just suppose he
        throws out all the medications
        and once again enjoys a medicine chest
        with only tooth paste, shaving cream and deodorant?

Just suppose he
        discards all charts
        disposes of the machines
                that tell of sugar and blood?

Jus suppose he
        does these things?

                (Maybe
                his eyes need
                to smile again.

                Will I
                smile back, and
                hold his hand?)

Lenses

It's anyone's guess
which lens she'll be wearing
today.

> (Or me, either,
> for that matter.)

Will it be the
the dull, gray lens of:

> *"Poor me! Why does this happen to me?"*
> *"If anything can go wrong, it will!"*
> *"What did I do wrong that*
> *God*
> *is punishing me like this?"*
> *"Nobody cares anymore."*

Or will it be
the brighter yellow or pink lens of:

> *"It's a pretty good day!"*
> *"Do you think we could _____ today?"*
> *"I feel fine today!"*
> *"Why don't you go out for a while?"*

I can't lay out *her* lenses
as I lay out her clothes or medications.

But I *can* pick out *my own!*

> *What color lens*
> *shall I look through*
> *this day?*

Let Me!

Let me
        complain
        explain
        be "disloyal"
        not understand
        cry
        maybe yell
            and, please,
            just-
            listen
                without
                telling me how to do it better
                or, I shouldn't let it get to me.

Let me
        cry
        and cry
        and then
        cry some more

            and, please,
            don't give me advice.

            Do pass the tissues
            and hold me, if you can.

And let me be.

            Please,
            if you can,
            just *be* with me.

Then,
I'll be able to go back.
Better.

Let Them!

Why

        can't people
        let them?

People

        let children help.
        "They're learning,"
        they say, with indulgent smiles.

Why

        can't they
        let one who is old, sick, maybe dying,
             help?
        And that with a grateful and knowing smile
             from each.

Sometimes
      one, who receives so much,
      needs to give-
            however slowly, painfully, ineptly,
            even messily.
      One *needs* to give.

Why
      can't we
      let them?

Why?

Lists

Every day I make lists:

> super market
> dry cleaner
> bills
> soccer game
> laundry
> office party

Whatever the day's odds and ends bring.

Now my lists are longer:

> doctor's appointments
> pharmacy
> checking to see that he's OK
> watching time for medicines
> picking up (returning) laundry

It seems life is
> *one long list of things*
> to fit into
> an already full day.

> If my life
> is not to harden into
> a treadmill of lists

> > *What might I do?*
> > *(say, to be sure of some fun?)*

Look at Me!

You seem to be saying:
"*Look at me!*"

It hurts my heart,
You, my fastidious father,
you drool.

"*Look at me!*"

It hurts my heart,
You, my intelligent father,
you don't make sense.

"*Look at me!*"

It hurts my heart.
You, my well-groomed father,
you are awry and askew.

"*Look at me!*"

It hurts my heart.
You, my well mannered father,
you slurp and spill and stain.

"*Look at me!*"

You are right, my father.
You need me
to look at YOU–
not at your mouth or clothes or hair,
not at the mess caused by your weakness,
but at YOU.
I will look at you.
Better–
I am looking at you,
Loving you.

Losing It

It's too much.
I lost it.
Yesterday I just lost it.

With family and job my life already is full.
Then my spouse's mother moved in,
announcing she has a terminal disease.
(No, she *won't* go to a doctor.)

Then my daughter was diagnosed with cancer.
She needs radiation and chemo.
Will I help with the pre-school children?
(She does go, but gets so sick.)

There's just not enough of me to go around.

I lost it, but good.
It was in the doctor's office.
I'm not sure I won't lose it again.

Well,
what if I do?

Making Nice

I try so hard to make nice.
I say nice things about how he looks.
I suggest nice things to do.
I bring nice things to be enjoyed.
I'M NICE! I AM!

and
it doesn't work.

He gets quiet.
He gets sullen.
He sighs and rolls his eyes.
He turns away.

Nothing
I do or say
pleases him.

In my own
heart of hearts,
why
do I
treat him this well?

Minuet

He's dancing a minuet.

Like it or not
      he's leading me
      in *his* minuet.

He dances close,
says something:
"I love you.
Always have, you know."
He dances away.

He dances close.
      "Look out for her.
      She's going to need you."
He dances away.
  A little longer this time.

He dances close.
      "Let your brother
      have-that thing-
      he's always liked."
He dances away.
  Yet a little longer.

He dances close.
      Holds my hand.
      Smiles.

Motherless

When my 96-year-old mother
        (now functioning at about a 3-year-old level)
asks for *her* mother
    I comfort her.
    My heart weeps
        —for her
        —for me.

It is as if
she is being
      un-born
as she becomes
      a lisping child
          chanting nursery rhymes
          counting proudly to 10
          forgetting how to dress
and asking for her mommy.

She doesn't respond
      when I call her Mom,
      when the children call her Gran.

She does respond
      when I call her
         "My precious child."
         "My little one."

I want my mommy, too.

                Sometimes
                we both hug teddy bears.

My Feet

I'm tired.

My feet hurt.

If only
I could walk with my seat
and sit on my feet
It would help.

Mystery

Doctors say:

"Every body is different.
We'll try this and
wait and see how your body responds."

Maybe it will help.
Maybe not.
Bodies, with all their peculiarities,
are full of mystery.

Hearts, even more so.

Who knows all of the heart's secrets?
Who know, down deep, why they (or we)
do what we do?

Who truly knows (even of ourselves)
how we got to be
the way we are-
and can explain it?

And as we age
it only gets "more so!"

So much mystery!

When facing each other's mystery,
(theirs and my own)
I think of my grandfather's saying:

"Yep.
We're all crazy,
but in different ways."

No More

I ask what she thinks about something.
  She tells me how her knee is hurting.

I ask her what she thinks I should do about something.
  She complains about an annoying phone call.

I tell her what upset me that afternoon.
  She asks me to fix the TV.

I confide something which frightens me.
  She whines about the weather.

No more is she
as she used to be.

It takes a mighty lot of doing
(salted by my tears of grief and hurt)
to get used to
"no more is she ...."

Except my loving her.
And, probably,
she, me.

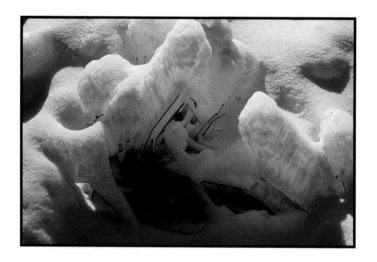

No One Knows

And no one would believe me
if they heard me say:
    "No one knows."

Family, other relatives, friends-
all come around,
and help.
    They chat.
    They are sympathetic.
    They praise me.

But-
    No one *listens.*
    No one *sees* below the surface.
    No one *knows* what it is like for me
        or of the complex bundle in my heart.
    No one *understands.*

It might sound crazy
to say-
in the middle of this big family,
    many friends and good people:

        I AM SO LONELY!
        I AM SO ALONE!
        I AM HOLLOW INSIDE!

The "I" of me
is anonymous.
Invisible.
Neither noticed nor cared for.

Isn't there *anyone*
who will listen
with loving intelligence?

... and ...
just *know?*

Now!

Once
> on a dark and cold winter's evening
> a holy man of God
> jabbed his cigarette into the top button of my coat,
> demanding:

> *"What have you got to give God?"*

Apparently
> He knew THE answer.

It was too cold
> to play "twenty questions,"

So I asked,
> *"What?"*

"NOW!"
> he shouted.

Withdrawing his cigarette he continued:

> *"This moment.*
> *The past is gone.*
> *You don't know the future.*
> *NOW!"*

Now *is* all I have
> for God, for me,
> or for anyone else.

> > How might I
> > go about
> > ENJOYING my
> > now -ing?

Paper Work

Paper Work!

What fills my mail box?
>   *Paper Work!*

What floods my living space?
>   *Paper Work!*

What contains sneaky, troublesome fine print?
>   *Paper Work!*

What takes every spare moment (and hours I cannot afford!)
>   *Paper Work!*

What brings worrisome bills,
>   outrageous bills,
>   bills not our bills?
>   *Paper Work!*

>   Is there no relief from
>   *Paper Work!*

>   I need to go for a long walk.
>   Or take a long bubble bath
>   (with music).

Please Don't!

To some of you
well-meaning callers
I want to **shout:**
"Please don't!"

Please don't
come in, hear us, then respond with:
"I know someone who
has it worse than you."
(I don't want to hear about
"someone."
I want you to hear about *us.*)

Please don't
come in and say:

"If only he would visualize, then ...
"If only he would use alternative medicine, then ...
"If only he would follow this diet, then ...
"If only he would ... ."

Please don't!

You overwhelm him (and me).
You make it seem as if he doesn't get well
it is his fault. Or mine.

It isn't!

Please do
be with us,
as we are,
now.

That's what I want to shout, to some people, these days.

A Puzzle

It's a puzzle.

I haven't been able to get a hold of it.

What *can* she do?
What can she *really not* manage?

When is she playing on my sympathy?
When is she, stubbornly, doing too much?

How can she say those things?
Does she know what she is doing?

How much is really deliberate, conscious?
How much is "left over" fragments of what was?
                    —or, what are the now fears?

It's a puzzle.

> *Maybe it's meant to be a puzzle.*
> *Maybe it's as puzzling to her as to me.*

> *What can I do? No,*
> *How can I be for her?*
> *and for myself and the rest of us?*

> *How can I be*
> *my true self, now?*

Reality

Reality **is.**
>   Whatever it *is*
>   However it *is*
Reality **is.**

>   How I respond to it,
>   what I do about,
>   That is another matter.

When I pretend reality **isn't**
>   (He *can* answer me ..."
>   (He *does not have to* soil himself")

>   I'm banging my head against a brick wall.
>   *My poor head!*

When I try to ignore reality
>   ("She will be all right left alone."
>   ("She will remember to take her medicine.")

>   I'm stubbing my big toe against a brick wall.
>   *My poor toe!*

When I expect them to be
>   the way they were

>   My pounding fist bleeds.
>   *My poor fist!*

When

>   *will I take better care of*
>   *my head, my toe, my fist,*
>   *me? ...*

>   *and them?*

Reciprocity

If

    I believe
    that all life is reciprocal

Then

    I can live off your strengths
    and help balance your weaknesses.

    As you do from and for me.

The way

    we used to do this
    (even if not consciously)
    suited us then.

The way

    we need to do it now
    suits us today.

    Things have changed
    a great deal
    to require this
    new "suiting."

    May I grow
    to make a good fit!

Ruined!

My life is ruined.
YES IT IS.

I never intended to spend these years
caregiving like this.

Well,
they say to me:

"Perhaps your life merely
is interrupted.
It can't last forever."

If so,
when it is over,
I most certainly will
make up for all this wasted time!

OOPS!

Do I want these years
to be no more than
"ruined", "interrupted", "wasted"?

Not good enough!
Not good enough at all!

Sleep

What a great,
wonderful
self-repairing
self-giving
gift
is sleep!

One might even
(if one dares)
call sleep
"One of God's
better ideas."

But sleep,
like so many things
these days
doesn't get the time
it deserves.

May sleep,
like my other good friends,
know I treasure her,
and know that
we shall get together
more often and longer again,
when other things allow.

Smelling the Roses

"Stop and smell the roses,"
they say.

"Sure!"
I answer.

Then–I did.

She received a bouquet from a friend.
The roses are on her bed table.

She was dozing off.

I had time to wait.

Her room mate was sleeping, too.

Instead of reading,
I looked at the roses.

Smelled them, too,
but mostly looked.

In the looking
I saw the unfolding.

In the unfolding
I saw the heart.

It made me wonder,
and it filled me with awe
at the beauty of
        unfolding,
        revealing the heart.

When she awakened,
she smiled.

And now I can, too.
From my heart.

So Hurt!

Sometimes (like now)
> I just about *hate* my brother.

I'm the one who takes care of Mom,
> day in and day out:
> bathing her, cleaning, doing laundry,
> cooking for her.

He came in on a Sunday,
> fussed over her,
> called her "my girl,"
> made her laugh.
Then he disappeared.

I'm the one
> who takes her to the doctors.

He came in after work on a Tuesday,
> sympathized with her complaints
> > (mostly about me),
> patted her hair,
> called her outrageous love names.
Then he disappeared.

I'm the one
> who does the unending medical insurance forms,
> argues with customer service over wrong billing,
> pays what needs be paid.

He came in, humming, on a Saturday afternoon,
> with a flower
> just for "my girl."
Then he disappeared.

I'm the one who
      changes the dressings,
      keeps track of the meds,
      cleans up her messes.

He came in, smiling, yesterday,
      telling me she just changed her will.
      He gets all, (not much, but all)
      because *he* is so good to her.

              I made him leave.
              I'm still crying.

Strange

I'm noticing something *strange*.

He I am-
>   trying
>   to balance the
>   bowling balls of my life.

Her I am-
>   struggling
>   to get everything done.

Here I am-
>   attempting
>   to "live one day at a time."

>   And what happens?

People-
>   people I know, and
>   some I hardly know, both,
>   "want to talk."

Strange!
>   *They* "want to talk" to *me,* and talk
>   about such personal things.
>   *To me!*

Not only that,
We both
get something out of it!

>   Actually, it's rather comforting.

Talkers

Oh,
can she talk!
And talk and talk and talk!

Guinness World Records
might well be interested in her!

Why visit?
Why bother?
It doesn't do any good.

Or,
does it?

Whose needs
am I looking at?
Hers? Mine?

If *her* needs
are my real concern-

May she talk and talk and talk
And talk and talk and talk.

(Perhaps I can put my need
"to get a word in edgewise"
into a box,
wrapped and ribboned,
given as a gift
from my heart.)

Teaching My Child

I will teach my child:
- to make plans
- to keep promises
  but also
- to hold them respectfully and lightly; and
- to change them generously,
  when there is need.

I will teach my child:
- what not and
- what to expect from life; and
- to receive it all (lovely and unpleasant alike)
  with a glad gratitude.

I will teach my child:
neither to be repulsed by
nor to fear
what birth, illness, accident, aging
    can do to bodies and minds;
and to accept change
as a normal part of life.

I will teach my child:
    that becoming who one is meant to be
        often requires discipline, sometimes harsh;
    that there is no other way
        to learn to be fully human.

I shall teach my child:
    to be realistic in mind and body;
        graciously, humorously, generously realistic.

I shall teach my child:
    to enjoy LIFE, *all* of it!

    ... in the teaching
    may I, too, learn!

Tenderness

Tenderness
has a new meaning for me
as I visit these two people.

They are long in love,
long married,
and now ...
one has a very short time to live.
The other is disabled.

He used to care for her,
doing what she could not do.
Now she does the caring-for,
struggling physically with the simplest tasks
while he watches–
in anguish, pity, helplessness, love.

The tenderness between them
lives, glows, weeps–and loves anew.

That's Done!

Small satisfactions
    bring much pleasure.

"That's done!"
One more thing crossed off the list.

        I love crossed-off things on lists!
        (Sometimes I put little things
        on the list,
        just so I can
        cross them off!)

When all
(well, most)
are crossed off

I take the time
for ...
        a cup of coffee
        a long bath
        a crossword puzzle
        reading something silly.

        (Maybe these sorts of things
        should go on my list!)

They Want

They want ...

    —my family wants
    —my friends want
    —the hospital wants
    —the insurance people want.

They have a right to want.
I should give them
      what they want.

        My body is tired.
        My mind is in a fog.

I want-
these tired days-
I want
     it to be over.

        There!
        I said it!
        I want it to be over!
        (ought I feel guilty?)

As the fog lifts
(a little)
I ask:
     How can I meet
     all of these wants?

        How can I, in their midst,
        live in peace?

They're Not
My Parents Anymore

I don't know them anymore.

I never saw that behavior before.
I never heard that foul language before.
I never endured that silence (or screeching) before.

They're different people.
They're not my parents anymore.

But–
they are.

Every so often
I see a flicker in their eyes–
a puzzling, questioning, flicker.

I know what it's like for me.
What must it be like for them?

How will I let it affect me
in the deepest part
of my heart?

UN-

I feel full of
    UN's:

    un - seen
    un - known
    un - attended
    un - appreciated
    un - accompanied
    un - cared for.

If I think about it,
    I might even find
    some more un's!

        How I wish
        a Good Samaritan
            would come along
            and see me!

        If someone were
        to see me,
        compassionately acknowledge my struggles
        perhaps I could change all of the un's
        to one:
                un-afraid!

Waiting

I hate waiting!
I don't have time to wait!
(But, if I leave, I'll only have to come back
and wait some more.)

I make the time to take him to the doctor.
I need to
get back to work myself
be home when the baby-sitter has to leave
make arrangements with the plumber
(can't go on with the toilet the way it is!).

Now the doctor is late. Very late.

Does the receptionist,
who has to cover for him, of course,
treat us in, oh, *so soothing* a fashion.
It's almost as if she were saying,
"There, there. Now, now.
Be good."

I can just about feel her patting my head.
I bristle
(My head never liked being patted.)

We wait.
Waiting is becoming
my most unfavorite thing.

Boo hoo!

Wasting Time

They call and call.
They visit and visit.
They ask and ask:

> "How is she doing?"
> "What does the doctor say?"
> "What's happening?"

I waste so much time telling the same things
            over and
            over and
            over again.
(Maybe I could make a weekly tape!)

On the other hand:

> If no one called, or
> If no one visited, or
> If no one asked,
> I'd be even more upset.
> (and so would she!)

Sometimes

> I think
> I don't know
> *what* I want.
> I'm too tired

> > wasting time
> > answering the same questions
> > over and over, and over again!

And then
I wonder:

Is it truly wasting time?
How much poorer might I (we) be
without this *wasted* time?

What If?

There's nothing like the
What if's ...
to scare me.

What if–
    our savings run out?

What if–
    they take the kids' college money?

What if–
    it gets so bad I can't provide adequate care?

What if–
    we lose the house? Or even the car?

What if–
    I get sick ... or

What if–
    I die first?

      On the other hand,

      What if
      we really make a go of it?
      (We've done that before
      and are rather good at it!)

What I Want

When I tell you my troubles-
        what's so disgusting, frustrating
                and expensive
        what's so relentlessly wearing
        what's so hopeless-

I want
        you
        to companion my heart.

I do NOT want
        advice
        a story about "I know someone who ..."
        a pious admonition
        you to change the subject.

I want you
        to know what it's like for me,
                judging neither them nor me,
        just-
        knowing what it's like for me.

Can you,
        will you,
        do that for me?

Please?

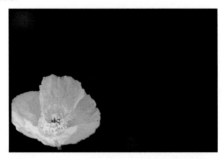

What Must I Do?

My life
is threatened.

She needs care.
There is no question about it.

I have responsibility.
There is no question about it.

Must I be the one
to take care of her?

She thinks so!
So do her friends.

Must I?

> It isn't just the inconvenience
> or the change in my (family's) life style
> or even the expense.

> It is how she is
> (and always was)
> disruptive, nasty, demanding,
> setting family members against each other.

> I-we-
> see her coming
> as most harmful to us.

What must I do?

> *Another form of tough love?*
> *Perhaps manage her care, but*
> *not do it directly?*
> *Or ... ?*

Whiny, Whiny

He expects something-
      It's more than I can do.

I expect something-
      It's more than he can do.

So we, each in our own way,
    whine:
        "You're selfish!"
        "How insensitive of you!"
        "You don't know what I'm going through!"
        "You don't care."

To anyone who will listen
    (or whom we can entrap),
we whine.

      How might we
      come to *feel for* each other?
      (or at least I for her?)

      And if
      "I'm the one who always gives in,"

      why might (not)
      I be willing to do so this time?

Afterword

No matter your relationship to the one for whom you are proving care (spouse, parent, sibling, child, friend, stranger), all caregivers have some things in common.

First comes the great commandment of love of neighbor. But do attend to the wording of it: LOVE YOUR NEIGHBOR *AS YOURSELF.*

You can't give what you don't have.

Love yourself: well, appropriately. (We get so afraid of being called-or being-selfish.) There is a healthy self-love for which English does not have a good word.

All of us, but most especially caregivers, need to learn to take care of their own person: to feed their own bodies and souls.

Often this involves something many of us find difficult: ASKING FOR HELP. When much caring is needed, much help is needed. You probably cannot do it alone. Please find ways to ask for, and receive, help.

Then there is dealing with life's deepest questions. Many self-help books are inadequate to this life task. When it comes to this level of decision about the kind of human being each of us is, or want to become, NO ONE and NOTHING can provide the answers for another. That is work we each need to do for ourselves. It comes from the deepest places in our heart. The place where we meet our God-where our truest self resides.

One of the richest rewards of caregiving is its most demanding: To know ourselves, to face ourselves, to decide who and what the *self* truly is. (not our words, not our titles or possession or roles, but our SELF).

You might be thinking: Sure, but why force this work on top of everything else caregiving demands? Well, maybe because caregiving is the occasion for our growing true. One thing is almost sure: It will make us or break us as persons.

That is why many reflections in this small book end with questions. The answers are in you. Your growth in wisdom is crucial.

May you find deep satisfaction and joy in your decisions!